FORERUNNERS: IDEAS FIRST FROM THE UNIVERSITY OF
MINNESOTA PRESS

Original e-works to spark new scholarship

FORERUNNERS IS A thought-in-process series of breakthrough digital
works. Written between fresh ideas and finished books, Forerunners
draws on scholarly work initiated in notable blogs, social media,
conference plenaries, journal articles, and the synergy of academic
exchange. This is gray literature publishing: where intense thinking,
change, and speculation take place in scholarship.

D1371929

Ian Bogost
The Geek's Chihuahua: Living with Apple

Andrew Culp
Dark Deleuze

Grant Farred
Martin Heidegger Saved My Life

Gary Hall
The Uberfication of the University

John Hartigan
Aesop's Anthropology: A Multispecies Approach

Mark Jarzombek
Digital Stockholm Syndrome in the Post-Ontological Age

Nicholas A. Knouf
How Noise Matters to Finance

Akira Mizuta Lippit
Cinema without Reflection: Jacques Derrida's Echopoiesis and Narcissism Adrift

Reinhold Martin
Mediators: Aesthetics, Politics, and the City

Shannon Mattern
Deep Mapping the Media City

Jussi Parikka
The Anthrobscene

Steven Shaviro
No Speed Limit: Three Essays on Accelerationism

Sharon Sliwinski
Mandela's Dark Years: A Political Theory of Dreaming

The Uberfication of the University

The Uberfication
of the University

Gary Hall

University of Minnesota Press

MINNEAPOLIS

Published by the University of Minnesota Press, 2016
111 Third Avenue South, Suite 290
Minneapolis, MN 55401-2520
http://www.upress.umn.edu

Fuck off and die—and not in that order.

—Then London mayor BORIS JOHNSON, speaking to a
London taxi driver during a row over Uber, June 5, 2015

Contents

Preface   xi

The Sharing Economy   1

Platform Capitalism   7

Uber.edu   15

The Reputation Economy   23

The Microentrepreneur of the Self   30

The Para-academic   39

The Artrepreneur   44

Affirmative Disruption   48

Postscript   54

Acknowledgments   57

Preface

AT FIRST the 2008 financial crisis looked as if it was going to constitute a major threat to the long-term viability of neoliberalism. Viewed from our current vantage point, however, it seems merely to have given the champions of the free market an opportunity to carry out with increased intensity their program of privatization, deregulation, and reduction to a minimum of the state, public sector, and welfare system. The result is a condition we can describe as postwelfare capitalism.

The Uberfication of the University explores what neoliberalism's further weakening of the social is likely to mean for the future organization of labor by examining data and information companies associated with the emergence of the corporate sharing economy. It focuses on the sharing economy because it is here that the implications for workers of such a shift to a postwelfare capitalist society are most apparent today. This is a society in which we are encouraged to become not just what Michel Foucault calls *entrepreneurs of the self* but *microentrepreneurs of the self,* acting as if we are our own, precarious, freelance microenterprises in a context in which we are being steadily deprived of employment rights, public services, and welfare support. Witness the description one futurologist gives of how the nature of work will change, given that 30 to 80 percent of all jobs are predicted to disappear in the next twenty years as a result of developments in automation and advanced robotics: "You might be driving Uber part of the day, renting out your spare bedroom on Airbnb a little bit, renting out space in your closet as storage for Amazon or housing the drone that does delivery for Amazon."[1]

The book analyzes the implications of this transformation to a postwelfare capitalist society for the organization of labor largely through the prism of those who work and study in the university. It does so partly because academics, researchers, and students *are* now being encouraged to become microentrepreneurs of themselves and of their own lives—so even so-called good jobs are being affected—but mainly because the university provides one of the few spaces in postindustrial society where the forces of contemporary neoliberalism's anti-public sector regime are still being overtly opposed, to a certain extent at least.[2] It follows that such changes in the way labor is organized will be all the more powerfully and visibly marked in the case of the publicly funded and legally nonprofit university system. Indeed if, as research reveals, being an academic is one

1. Rohit Talwar, futurologist and CEO of Fast Future Research, quoted in Nicola Slawson, "Today's Pupils 'Could Still Be Working at 100,'" *Guardian,* October 7, 2015, 5.

2. Higher education is not the only place where neoliberalism is, for the moment, being resisted. There are those who place faith in the ability of the unions to form a counterhegemonic block, while in the United Kingdom, the National Health Service and the BBC are still publicly owned institutions delivering much-valued public services—although the latter is more in the position of holding back the tide than actively resisting, being even more of an establishment institution than the university in some respects, many of its governors, managers, and employees having the same ideas about politics, business, and the world as conservative neoliberals.

of the most desired jobs in Britain today, it may be precisely because this occupation is seen as offering a way of living, of being alive, that is *not* just about consuming and working and very little else.[3]

3. "YouGov research reveals that the most desired jobs in Britain are not what you might expect; they are not even the most reliably well paid ones. . . . Being an author is the number one most desired job in Britain. Not only would the most people like to be one (60%), the smallest percentage would not like to be one (32%). The only other jobs preferred by a majority are equally as bookish: librarian (54%) and academic (51%)." Will Dahlgreen, "Bookish Britain: Literary Jobs Are the Most Desirable," YouGov UK, February 15, 2015, https://yougov.co.uk/news/2015/02/15/bookish-britain-academic-jobs-are-most-desired/.

The Sharing Economy

TALK ABOUT BEING CAREFUL WHAT YOU WISH FOR: a recent survey of university vice-chancellors in the United Kingdom identifies a number of areas of innovation with the potential to reshape higher education. Among them are "uses of student data analytics for personalized services" (the number one innovation priority for 90 percent of vice-chancellors); "uses of technology to transform learning experiences" (massive open online courses [MOOCs]; mobile virtual learning environments [VLEs]; "anytime-anywhere learning" (leading to the demise of lectures and timetables); and "student-driven flexible study modes" ("multiple entry points" into programs, bringing about an end to the traditional academic year).[1] Responding to this survey, an editorial in the academic press laments that "the UK has world-leading research universities, but what it doesn't have is a higher education equivalent of Amazon or Google, with global reach and an aggressive online strategy."[2] Yet

---

1. PA Consulting Group, *Lagging Behind: Are UK Universities Falling Behind in the Global Innovation Race?,* June 18, 2015, http://www.paconsulting.com/our-thinking/higher-education-report-2015/#here.

2. John Gill, "Losing Our Place in the Vanguard?," *Times Higher Education,* June 18, 2015, 5, https://www.timeshighereducation.co.uk/opinion/losing-our-place-vanguard.

one wonders whether any of those proclaiming the merits of such disruptive innovation have ever stopped to consider what a higher education institution emulating the expansionist ambitions of U.S. companies like Amazon and Google would actually mean for those currently employed in universities.

We can see the impact such aggressive, global, for-profit technology companies have on the organization of labor by looking at information and data analytics businesses associated with the sharing economy. Emerging from the mid-2000s onward, the sharing economy is a socioeconomic ecosystem that supplies individuals with information that makes access to things like ridesharing and sofa surfing possible on a more efficient, expanded basis. Indeed, because of the emphasis that is placed on the cooperative sharing and renting of preowned and unused goods, the activities and services of the sharing economy are frequently held as being very different from, or as even as offering an alternative to, those that are provided through private, state, or public channels. As such, the sharing economy is portrayed as a means of bringing community values back into the ways in which people consume. It is also said to help address environmental issues resulting from the depletion of the planet's resources, for example, by reducing the carbon footprint of transport. Yet the sharing economy is just part of a much larger socioeconomic ecosystem, one that is dominated by the use of computing and satellite technology to coordinate workforces and create global transnational supply chains and that enables just-in-time manufacturing through the production of low-wage labor and the exploitation of outsourced workers. Given this, it is almost as if the sharing economy has been devised to take the edge off some of the harsher aspects of life in advanced, postindustrial capitalist society, including those that have been generated in the name of austerity: unemployment, precarity, increasing income inequality, large discrepancies in property ownership, high levels of debt, and low levels of class mobility.

Certain aspects of the sharing economy, however, are also helping to enact a significant societal shift. It is a shift in which state-regulated service intermediaries, such as taxi companies and hotels, are replaced by information and data management intermediaries, such as the start-ups Uber (an app that enables passengers to use their cell phones to hail a ride with a taxi, rideshare, or private car) and Airbnb (a community marketplace for renting out private lodging and other kinds of accommodation that, like Uber, was founded in San Francisco).[3] Of course, it is important to acknowledge that the sharing economy is made up of a variety of different economic arrangements, many of which are not directly involved in the replacement of state-regulated service intermediaries. These arrangements embrace for-profit, nonprofit, and collaborative structures too: those associated with fair trade collectives, freecycling networks, peer-to-peer file sharing, and the Occupy movements, for example. Even the information and data management intermediaries of the sharing economy—which include BlaBlaCar, Liquid, and Zaarly, among many others too numerous to mention—are not all the same. Each has its own specific features, characteristics, and spheres of operation within the larger ecosystem of the sharing economy. Nevertheless, rather than sharing activities, goods, and services in a fair and resilient fashion that enables a more direct exchange between the parties involved by cutting out the

3. Evgeny Morozov, "What You Whistle in the Shower: How Much for Your Data?," *Le Monde Diplomatique,* English edition, August 2014, posted on the nettime mailing list by Patrice Riemens, August 24, 2014, https://www.mail-archive.com/nettime-l@mail.kein.org/msg02769 .html.

unnecessary middlemen, what most of these for-profit start-ups are doing is corporatizing and selling cheap and easy-to-access assets that are underutilized. In the case of Uber and Airbnb, still the two best-known examples, these assets take the form of seats in vehicles and rooms in properties that are otherwise occupied on an infrequent and temporary basis. In other words, they are idle resources it has up until now been difficult for capital to commodify and whose value from an entrepreneurial point of view has therefore been wasted.

For some, this move away from state-regulated service inter-mediaries such as taxi companies and hotels toward for-profit businesses is part of market capitalism's increasing co-option and rebranding of the "true" community values of the sharing economy. Even if this form of economy is presented as a revival of community spirit, it actually has very little to do with *sharing* access to goods, activities, and services and everything to do with *selling* this access. (Many people insist on referring to it not as the sharing economy but as the *renting economy* for just this reason.) The sharing economy thus does hardly anything to challenge inequality and injustice. At best, it is capable of providing an additional or alternative source of income in what many are experiencing as economically straightened times. (It is significant that Uber and Airbnb were both founded around the time of the financial crisis, in 2009 and 2008, respectively.) For others, these technology start-ups are simply innovating too quickly for the politicians and lawmakers to keep pace—a situation regarded as likely to have highly disruptive social con-sequences if it continues unconstrained.[4]

4. See Sebastian Olma, "Never Mind the Sharing Economy: Here's Platform Capitalism," Institute of Network Cultures, October 16, 2014, http://networkcultures.org/mycreativity/2014/10/16/never-mind-the-sharing-economy-heres-platform-capitalism/; Yochai Benkler, "Challenges of the

But this societal shift from state-regulated service intermediaries to information and data analytics intermediaries also provides us with a means of understanding some of the ways in which neoliberalism has been able to advance with its program of privatization, deregulation, and reduction to a minimum of the role played by the state and public sector even after the crash of 2008. The important point to note in this respect is that, by avoiding preemptive state regulation, these profit-driven sharing economy businesses are operating according to a *postwelfare model of capitalism.* Here there are few legislative protections for workers and hardly any possibilities for establishing trade unions or other forms of collective agency, action, or means of generating the kind of solidarity that might be able to challenge this state of affairs. This set of circumstances often leaves those who provide services by means of the platforms of information and data management intermediaries laboring for less than the minimum wage and without a host of workers' rights (a bundle of rights being what employment is, after all). The list of lost benefits is a long one. As Mike Bulajewski notes, it includes "the right to have employers pay social security, disability, and unemployment insurance taxes, the right to family and medical leave, workers' compensation protection, sick pay, retirement benefits, profit sharing plans, protection from discrimination on the basis of race, color, religion, sex, age or national origin, or wrongful termination for becoming pregnant, or reporting sexual harassment or other types of employer wrongdoing."[5] All of this goes a long way to explain why in

Shared Economy," World Economic Forum, February 24, 2015, https://www.youtube.com/watch?v=mBF-GFDaCpE.

5. Mike Bulajewski, "The Cult of Sharing," *Mrteacup: A Blog of Philosophical Reflections and Speculations,* August 5, 2014, http://www.mrteacup.org/post/the-cult-of-sharing.html.

the March 2015 budget, the British government declared that it is planning to make the United Kingdom a global center for the sharing economy.[6] (Uber was declared legal in the United Kingdom in October 2015.)

6. "Support for the Sharing Economy," in H. M. Treasury, Budget 2015, section 1.193, https://www.gov.uk/government/uploads/system/uploads/attachment_data/file/416330/47881_Budget_2015_Web_Accessible.pdf.

Platform Capitalism

IT IS NO SURPRISE that one of the other names associated with this aspect of the sharing economy is "platform capitalism." As Sebastian Olma points out, building on the work of Sascha Lobo, this is the term given to the "generic 'ecosystem'" in which a software-driven environment such as eBay or TaskRabbit, rather than simply acting as a marketplace for connecting customers to companies, is "able to link potential customers to anything and anyone, from private individuals to multinational corporations." In platform capitalism, then, "everyone can become a supplier for all sorts of products and services at the click of a button."[1] Indeed, if neoliberalism can be understood as trying to introduce market rationality into all areas of society, the for-profit sector of the sharing economy appears as almost the neoliberal ideal. It creates a situation in which the general population not only as-

1. Olma, "Never Mind the Sharing Economy." See also Sascha Lobo, "Die Mensch-Maschine: Auf dem Weg in die Dumpinghölle," *Der Spiegel,* September 3, 2014, http://www.spiegel.de/netzwelt/netz politik/sascha-lobo-sharing-economy-wie-bei-uber-ist-plattform -kapitalismus-a-989584.html. For more on the politics of platforms, see the "Platform Politics" issue of *Culture Machine* 13 (2014), http://www .culturemachine.net/index.php/cm/issue/view/25.

pires to own their own homes—the vision the conservative prime minister Margaret Thatcher sold to the British working classes in the 1980s with the right-to-buy scheme (itself designed as a means of reducing the role played by the state in the form of collectively owned social housing)[2]—but also have the opportunity to become private capitalist entrepreneurs and economic agents themselves. And in the case of Airbnb, one way in which they can do so is precisely by trading otherwise underutilized space in their now *privately owned* homes. As the company's cofounder and CEO, Brian Chesky, proclaims, previously, "only businesses could be trusted, or people in your local community. Now, that trust has been democratized—any person can act like a brand. . . . It means that people all over a city, in 60 seconds, can become microentrepreneurs."[3]

The information and data management intermediaries of the sharing economy may create jobs, then, but "it's a new kind of job," as Chesky readily acknowledges. "Maybe it's like a 21st-century job," he suggests. Or maybe, given the lack of workers' rights and degree of externalized risk, it's like a very old kind of job: a Victorian, nineteenth-century job.[4] For these companies, and the microentrepreneurs who labor for them—and who in the past would have been known as *employees*—are operating in an open market that is relatively free from the ability of state regulators, the labor movement, and trade unions not only to

2. Whereas 42 percent of the U.K. population lived in a council house in 1979, today that number is less than 8 percent.

3. Brian Chesky, interview by Rik Kirkland in "The Future of Airbnb in Cities," McKinsey & Company, November 2014, http://www.mckinsey.com/Insights/Travel_Transportation/The_future_of_Airbnb_in_cities?cid=other-eml-alt-mip-mck-oth-1411. It is worth noting that Chesky's last point is not strictly correct: more often than not, you need to have an asset—be it property, a car, or time—to be in a position to "share."

4. Ibid.

put a limit on the maximum hours those employed in these new kinds of jobs work in a day or week but also to specify the minimum wage they should receive, the number of days off they need, and the paid holidays and free weekends they are entitled to.[5] It is *as if* many of these means of taking a break from work and having some downtime are now to be provided by the for-profit sharing economy businesses themselves—along with other companies with an investment in the management of information and data (and the aggressive avoidance of tax), such as Apple and Google (or Alphabet, as the search engine's parent company is now called)—through their ability to save people's time and complete tasks for them. To provide just one example that is today already commonplace, consider the linking of users' electronic diaries to their e-mail accounts and sending of automatic calendar appointment and "to-do" list reminders to them on their cell phones. (From June 2012, the Reminders app has come with every Apple device running iOS 5 or above, while the ColorNote app for Android has been downloaded 80 million times since it was launched in 2009.) It won't be too long before phones and watches are scheduling meetings and

5. What is more, like many neoliberal businesses, these information and data management intermediaries continue to have a parasitical relationship with the state at the same time as they argue against it and its regulation. For example, while Chesky argues for the modernization—which in this context is nearly always a code word for neoliberalization—of "outdated" state legislation and laws that restrict what is possible when a person acts like a brand, he nevertheless goes on to acknowledge of Airbnb that "the reason it's grown so fast is, unlike traditional businesses, we don't have to pour concrete. The infrastructure and the investment was already made by cities a generation ago. And so all of a sudden, all you needed was the internet." Ibid. It is an Internet, one might add, which was itself the product of state funding for research, education, and technological development, namely, that behind CERN.

sending replies *for* people, with driverless cars that can be summoned by smartwatch predicted to be just fifteen years away. The "taptic engine" feature of the Apple Watch means users don't even have to spend time taking their phones out of their pockets to know they've received a message: the watch just gives them a gentle tap on the wrist. Given that a study finds the average user picks up her phone eighty-five times a day, amounting to approximately one-third of the time she is awake, this represents a not inconsiderable saving.[6] Yet a question can be raised as to whether these companies and their products *are* saving people's time or whether they are actually enabling them to work even more. A survey of fifteen hundred senior staff released by the Chartered Manager's Institute in 2016, for instance, reveals that they spend a total of twenty-nine days a year working on smartphones and tablets outside of working hours. That's the equivalent of most employees' annual holiday allowance. No wonder the mode of production we appear to be moving toward has been described as not quite capitalism as it is classically understood but as "something worse."[7] Or that some tech workers are temporarily unplugging from electronic communications and putting their phones into flight mode as a means of gaining relief from the stress of having to answer e-mails and check Twitter constantly (and concentrate

6. "How We Use Our Smartphones Twice as Much As We Think," Lancaster University, October 29, 2015, http://www.lancaster.ac.uk/news/articles/2015/how-we-use-our-smartphones-twice-as-much-as-we-think/; Sally Andrews, David A. Ellis, Heather Shaw, and Lukasz Piwek, "Beyond Self-Report: Tools to Compare Estimated and Real-World Smartphone Use," *PLoS One,* October 28, 2015, http://journals.plos.org/plosone/article?id=10.1371/journal.pone.0139004.

7. McKenzie Wark, "Digital Labor and the Anthropocene," *DIS Magazine,* http://dismagazine.com/disillusioned/discussion-disillusioned/70983/mckenzie-wark-digital-labor-and-the-anthropocene/.

all the better on developing the systems that so control them and everyone else).[8] Digital detox has even become something a luxury status symbol among celebrities, with the actor Eddie Redmayne admitting recently that he has swapped his smartphone for an old-fashioned handset that doesn't have an Internet connection.

Production and control, profit and risk, are not *shared* in this sector of the economy at all, then. It is the decentralized networks of users who benefit from the greater convenience and reduced prices afforded by the sharing economy and who help to build the platform by providing the aggregated input, data, and attention value that function to generate a market. Noticeably, these users do not form a social community in the manner they do on other kinds of digital platforms: Wikipedia, for example, or even Facebook. And this is despite the fact that the technology companies concerned often employ the language of grassroots movements when addressing them: when Uber tries to mobilize its app-enabled users to protest against attempts by the state and other representatives of the "old economy" (trade unions, city mayors, cab companies) to regulate it, for instance. What is more, because they never really own the products and services they are purchasing, these users are more susceptible to questionable practices on the part of the sharing economy's microentrepreneurs than would ordinarily be the case in a state-regulated market.

Meanwhile, it is the owners of the information and data management intermediaries who take the profits generated by financializing, corporatizing, and exploiting the "sharing" of goods and services between the users and microentrepreneurs that these owners enable by turning this exchange into a mar-

8. My thanks to Kathleen Fitzpatrick for this last point.

ket. Not surprisingly, the former tend to be well-funded *professional* entrepreneurs, as opposed to the more *amateur* microentrepreneurs who do a lot of the actual labor. The owners—who are small in number, any wealth generated thus being concentrated in the hands of relatively few—also centrally control the platform, software, algorithm, data, and associated ecosystem, deciding on pricing and wage levels, work allocation, standards, conditions, and preferred user and laborer profiles. This means that who *does* and *does not* get to work as a microentrepreneur in this economy is not delimited by state legislation or organized union activity designed to protect workers from being exploited and discriminated against. In fact, research on the sharing economy shows that a certain "homophily" occurs, by which it is often "similar 'types' of people [who] provide and use these services (in terms of class, education and race)," especially when a rating system is employed.[9] Uber, for example, enables both customers and drivers to rate one another and suspends drivers if their scores are not high enough. There is also reported to be a regular scarcity of female "drivers for hire" in many of the cities across the world in which Uber operates.

Finally, it is the often quite isolated microentrepreneurs (who can now be potentially "any person" rather than a specific set of formally contracted employees) who labor to provide these services in the market created by the platform on a freelance, low-paid, on-demand, and precarious basis; who take the risks associated with having lost their rights, benefits, and protection as employees in this "gig economy," as it

9. Moira McGregor, Barry Brown, and Mareike Glöss, "Disrupting the Cab: Uber, Ridesharing, and the Taxi Industry," *Journal of Peer Production,* no. 6 (January 2015), http://peerproduction.net/issues/issue-6-disruption-and-the-law/essays/disrupting-the-cab-uber-ridesharing-and-the-taxi-industry/.

is sometimes known; and who, depending on the particular platform, often face "increased surveillance, deskilling, casualization, and intensification" of their labor too.[10] Hence former U.S. secretary of labor Robert Reich's description of this economic model as less of a sharing economy and more of a "share-the-scraps economy": "the big money goes to the corporations that own the software. The scraps go to the on-demand workers."[11]

Of course, this four-part structure consisting of customers, owners, labor intermediaries, and workers has long been a feature of advanced capitalism. For twenty years and more, companies have been downsizing their role as employers by outsourcing work to independent contractors, freelancers, and temps, thus reducing costs by circumventing labor laws that establish minimum standards, with all the attendant consequences for staff income, conditions, rights, benefits, and pensions. After all, companies cannot be held responsible for people if they are not officially contracted as their employees. The dispute at the National Gallery in London over the outsourcing of visitor services is thus merely one of the more recent examples of this long-standing practice, the (failed) attempt to casualize academic work at Warwick University by outsourcing hourly paid staff to a company called Teach Higher another. What makes the corporate sharing economy significantly different in this respect is the following:

1. The intermediaries are no longer *agencies* for outsourced labor. Such agencies have been replaced by data-driven platforms or apps, making it difficult for workers to negotiate for better pay and conditions—you can't argue very easily with the logic of an algorithm.

10. Ibid.
11. Robert Reich, "The Share-the-Scraps Economy," *Robert Reich* (blog), February 22, 2015, http://robertreich.org/post/109894095095.

2. The customers and laborers are subject to monitoring, surveillance, and control on an individual, finely grained basis facilitated by the development of GPS-enabled location services and networked mobile media (smartphones, tablets, etc.).

3. Workers are not a coherent group of formally contracted *employees* (even if they are often managed as though they are) but can now be *anyone*. It is a state of affairs that has the effect of turning all of us into potential self-employed economic agents, as anyone can rent out spare capacity in her home or car.[12]

12. As we shall see in what follows, it is a state of affairs that also threatens to take us *beyond* even the level of potential disruption associated with what we might call the Warwick University–Teach Higher model of higher education. In this model, it is universities, not learners, who are purchasing casualized teaching services from intermediaries such as Teach Higher *on behalf of students as consumers*. It is also universities in this model that, with the encouragement of for-profit corporation education providers such as Pearson, are "unbundling" their different functions to be able to contract each of them out separately to agencies with the aim of using competition to improve efficiency. My thanks to John Holmwood for reminding me of the importance of this Warwick University–Teach Higher model to any account of the future of higher education.

Uber.edu

IN THE INTERESTS OF CAPITAL, the for-profit sharing economy can therefore be seen to be involved in the process whereby each of us is being transformed into a dispersed, atomized, precarious, freelance microentrepreneur. That said, concerns about the sharing economy are all too easy to push to the back of our minds when we're trying to find an inexpensive place to stay for a weekend break or calling a taxi to take us home from a friend's place late at night. Many women especially consider Uber to be safer than a minicab, with its unknown driver (although there have been complaints that the company could do more to ensure the safety of female passengers). Uber also has the advantage of costing less than a licensed taxi and being easier and more convenient than both. With Uber you can track your vehicle as it approaches in real time and so be sure you are getting into the right one. Others appreciate the freedom from having to deal with cash that Uber's frictionless digital payment system provides. It is only when we begin to think about these information and data management intermediaries from the point of view of a worker rather than a user, and consider their potential to disrupt our own sphere of employment—with the associated consequences for *our* job security, income, sick pay, retirement benefits, pensions, and, as we shall see, subjectivities—that the full implications of the shift to a socially weakened form of capitalism they are helping to enact are really brought home. So what *is* the potential effect of this transformation in the organization of labor on higher education?

In April 2015, LinkedIn, the social networking platform for professionals based in Mountain View, California, spent £1.5 billion purchasing Lynda.com (also based in California), a supplier of online consumer-focused courses. Although it does not address the sharing economy specifically, a report of this deal published shortly afterward in the U.S. *Chronicle of Higher Education* under the title of "How LinkedIn's Latest Move May Matter to Colleges" was quick to draw attention to its potential implications for higher education.[1] Of course, with its University Pages and University Rankings Based on Career Outcomes,[2] LinkedIn already has enough data to be able to provide the kind of detailed analysis of which institutions and courses are launching graduates into which jobs and long-term career trajectories that no single traditional university can hope to match—and that's *before* its purchase of Lynda.com. But what the piece in the *Chronicle* made clear is that, with LinkedIn's imminent transition into being both a social network *and* an actual *provider* of education, such data could easily be used to develop a successful information

---

1. Goldie Blumenstyk, "How LinkedIn's Latest Move May Matter to Colleges," *Chronicle of Higher Education,* April 17, 2015, http://chronicle.com/article/How-LinkedIn-s-Latest-Move/229441/. Although Blumenstyk does not discuss the sharing economy, the speculative scenario that follows was inspired in part by this article's reflections on some of the possible implications for higher education of LinkedIn's acquisition of Lynda.com.

2. http://blog.linkedin.com/2013/08/19/introducing-linkedin-university-pages/; https://www.linkedin.com/edu/rankings/us/undergraduate.

and data intermediary business model for higher education: if not next year, then certainly in the near future, and if not by LinkedIn, then by some other for-profit technology company (Uber or Academia.edu, say, the latter having a business plan that depends on its ability to exploit data flows related to research).[3] Such a model would be based on providing "transparent" information on a finely grained basis to employers, students, funding agencies, governments, and policy makers. This information would indicate which of the courses, classes, and possibly even teachers on any such educational "sharing economy" platform are better at enabling students from a given background to obtain a particular academic degree classification or other educational credential or qualification, make the successful transition to a desirable job or career, reach the top of a given profession in a particular town, city, or country, and so achieve a high level of job satisfaction, security, salary, income, and earning capacity over a specific period or even a lifetime. You know the kind of thing: if you liked reading this book by this author, then you might also like taking this undergraduate course at X college, and this master's course at Y, and applying for this starter post at company Z.

3. For one (uncritical) account of how the technology—including mobile apps, online assessments, and a blockchain system for recording all aspects of each transaction—already exists to make such an HE platform a reality, see "Uber-U Is Already Here," May 6, 2016, http://teachonline.ca/tools-trends/exploring-future-education/uber-u-already-here. For more on Academia.edu, see Gary Hall, "What Does Academia.edu's Success Mean for Open Access: The Data-Driven World of Search Engines and Social Networking," *Ctrl-Z: New Media Philosophy* 5 (2015), http://www.ctrl-z.net.au/journal/?slug=issue-5, and Janneke Adema and Gary Hall, eds., *Really, We're Helping to Build This ... Business: The Academia.edu Files* (London: Open Humanities Press, 2016), http://liquidbooks.pbworks.com/w/page/11135951/FrontPage.

It doesn't end there. The *Chronicle* article also detailed how, in 2014, LinkedIn bought a company called Bright. Bright has developed algorithms enabling it to match posts with applicants according to the latters' particular achievements, competencies, and skill sets. And it wouldn't be too difficult for a for-profit business, with the kind of data LinkedIn now has the potential to gather, to do much the same for employers and students—right down to the level of their salary expectations, extracurricular activities, "likes," or even reputational standing and degree of trustworthiness. This business could charge a fee for doing so, just as online dating agencies make a profit from introducing people with compatible personalities and interests as deduced by algorithms. It could then charge a further fee for making this ultra-detailed information and data available on a *live* basis in *real time*—something that would no doubt be highly desirable in today's "flexible economy," where many employers want to be able to draw from a pool of part-time, hourly paid, zero-hours and no-contract workers who are available "on tap," often at extremely short notice.[4] Moreover, feeding all the data gathered back into the system would mean the courses, curricula, and class content of any such educational data and information intermediary, along with their cost, could be continuously refined and so made highly responsive to student and employer needs at local, national, and international levels. More ominously still, given that it would be able to control the platform,

---

4. Alessandro Gandini reports that "a recent survey conducted by the Freelancers Union in partnership with Elance-oDesk, a major digital marketplace for contractors and freelancers worldwide, shows how 53 million Americans were generating some or their entire income earned in 2013 from freelancing, making up 34% of the entire American workforce." Alessandro Gandini, "Digital Work: Self-Branding and Social Capital in the Freelance Knowledge Economy," *Marketing Theory*, October 1, 2015.

software, data, and associated ecosystem, it is clear that such a platform capitalist higher education business would also have the power to decide who could be most easily seen and found in any such alternative market for education, much as Google does with its page ranking. (In April 2015, the European commission decided that Google *has* a case to answer regarding the possible abuse of its dominance of search through "systematically" awarding greater prominence to its own ads.)

Perhaps understandably, following all the furor over MOOCs, the *Chronicle*'s analysis of LinkedIn's acquisition of Lynda.com shied away from arriving at any overly pessimistic conclusions as to what all this may mean for higher education and its system of certification and credentialing. Nevertheless, if a company like LinkedIn made the decision to provide this level of finely grained information and data for its own unbundled, relatively inexpensive online courses (and perhaps any other nontraditional for-profit education providers that sign up with them), *but not for those offered by its more expensive market competitors in the public, nonprofit sector,* it would surely have the potential to be at least as disruptive as Coursera, Udacity, FutureLearn, and others have proven to be to date, if not considerably more so. For the kind of information about degrees and student final destinations, and ability to react to market changes any traditional bricks-and-mortar institution is capable of providing on its own would appear extremely unsophisticated, limited, and slow to compile by comparison. And lest the adoption by a for-profit sharing economy business of such an aggressive stance toward public universities seems unlikely, it is worth noting that Google maintains its dominance of search in much the same way. In the words of its chief research guru, Peter Norvig, the reason Google has a 90 to 95 percent share of the European market for search is not because it has better algorithms than Yahoo! and Bing but rather "it just has more data."[5] Indeed, one of the great myths about neoliberalism is that it strives to create competition on an open market. Yet, as the venture capitalist Peter Thiel, cofounder of PayPal and early Facebook investor, emphasizes in his book *Zero to One,* what neoliberal businesses actually want is to be a monopoly: to be so dominant in their areas of operation that they in fact escape the competition and become a market of one. "Competition," as Thiel puts it elsewhere, "is for losers."[6] As if to testify to this belief, LinkedIn was itself bought by Microsoft in mid-2016 for $26.2 billion.

Of course, as a consequence of neoliberalism's program of privatization, deregulation, reduction to a minimum of the public sector, and insistence that even publicly funded universities operate like businesses and embrace a lot of the same practices and value systems as for-profit corporations (despite that many are registered charities and therefore have education, not profit generation, as their primary function), large numbers of those who work in higher education already have temporary, fixed-term, part-time, hourly paid, zero-hour, and other forms of contingent positions that make it difficult for them to offer much by way of resistance to the erosion of their academic freedom and economic security. According to the American Federation of Teachers, "76% of the total faculty workforce is now in non-permanent posts and 70% of these are part time."[7]

5. Peter Norvig, speaking to Tim O'Reilly, quoted in Tim O'Reilly, "A Few Thoughts on the Nexus One," *Radar,* January 5, 2010, http://radar.oreilly.com/2010/01/the-nexus-one-vs-iphone.html.

6. Peter Thiel, "Competition Is for Losers," *Wall Street Journal,* September 12, 2014, http://www.wsj.com/articles/peter-thiel-competition-is-for-losers-1410535536.

7. See Mary O'Hara, "'I Feel Guilty Spending My Money on Food. That's How Low My Income Is,'" *Guardian,* November 17, 2015, 40.

Meanwhile a report by the University and College Union (UCU) finds that "54% of all academic staff, and 49% of teaching staff in UK universities are employed on insecure contracts," [8] with a UCU survey of twenty-five hundred casualized staff identifying one-third of those in universities as already experiencing difficulty paying household bills, while as many as one-fifth have problems finding enough money to buy food.[9] Yet if something along the lines of the preceding scenario regarding the development of a successful information and data intermediary business model for higher education *does* come to pass, it will without doubt have the effect of further disrupting the public, nonprofit university system—only this time by means of a profit-driven company operating according to a postwelfare capitalist *philosophy,* just as Uber is currently disrupting state-regulated taxi companies and Airbnb the state-regulated hotel industry. Increasing numbers of university workers will thus find themselves in a situation not dissimilar to that facing many cab drivers today. Instead of operating in a sector regulated by the state, they will have little choice but to sell their cheap and easy-to-access courses to whoever is prepared to pay for them in the "alternative" sharing economy education market created by platform capitalism. They too will become atomized, free-lance microentrepreneurs in business for themselves. And as

8. University and College Union, *Precarious Work in Higher Education: A Snapshot of Insecure Contracts and Institutional Attitudes,* April 14, 2016, https://www.ucu.org.uk/media/7995/Precarious-work-in -higher-education-a-snapshot-of-insecure-contracts-and-institutional -attitudes-Apr-16/pdf/ucu_precariouscontract_hereport_apr16.pdf.

9. University and College Union, *Making Ends Meet: The Human Cost of Casualisation in Post-Secondary Education,* May 21, 2015, http://www.ucu.org.uk/media/7279/Making-ends-meet---the-human -cost-of-casualisation-in-post-secondary-education-May-15/pdf/ucu _makingendsmeet_may15.pdf.

such, they will experience all the problems of deprofession-alization, precarity (in the sense of being unable to control or even anticipate their own future), and continuous performance monitoring by networked surveillance technologies that such an economy brings. Is this what vice-chancellors and university presidents actually want?

The Reputation Economy

THE SHARING ECONOMY thus intensifies the neoliberal belief in the power of markets that are unregulated and underregulated by the state to improve the efficiency of society's performance by using competition and consumer choice as a way of expressing public decisions—in this case, regarding the funding of higher education.[1] If you are a poor teacher in this economy, the market forces you to take responsibility for being so and either improve or quit. State regulation is unnecessary—as is institutional intervention. The same applies if you teach a subject that proves to be unpopular with students. (Any anger or critique is directed accordingly: inward onto the self rather than outward onto social, political, or economic factors. *It's not the system of higher education that's the problem; it's me!*) Indeed, the development of preemptive technologies means that in the future, the market may even be able to discipline and control you *before* you have done anything wrong—and, what's more, without you knowing it's doing so. Some employers are already rejecting job candidates based on the browser they use when electronically

---

1. Of course, these markets only *appear* to be unregulated and underregulated by the state. The state still defines the rules and limits of the market, protecting private property, financial assets, and so forth.

submitting their applications. This is because analysis of the relevant data has revealed to these companies that applicants who use a less common browser to do so statistically make for better employees. The Open University in the United Kingdom has even developed an algorithm capable of predicting a student's final grade based on her performance during just the first week of a degree course. Significantly, it takes into account factors such as "how enthusiastically students participate in online learning forums to improve their results."[2]

It is not hard to see where a situation of the kind sketched here is likely to lead. Among the finely grained data gathered by any such platform capitalist higher education business will almost certainly be student ratings of the performance of individual teachers as compared to their peers: not just the kinds of evaluations students already provide of their professors concerning how easy it is to get good feedback, marks, and grades in their classes, for example, or the extent to which they are *always on* and available to answer student questions and respond rapidly to queries by e-mail, Facebook, or text message, no matter what time of day or night it is, but also how good they are at adapting to the social and emotional needs of students—even how upbeat, friendly, and fun they are (in the way Uber drivers are expected to be *chatty*).

According to research commissioned by the UCU in 2013, increasing numbers of U.K. academics are experiencing problems of mental health. No doubt belonging to a profession that attracts overachievers does not help. Nor does the fact that performance indicators encouraging self-monitoring, self-assessment, and self-comparison are more or less built into the

---

2. "The Week in Higher Education," *Times Higher Education,* July 13, 2015, 4.

career trajectory. Academics learn very early on just what kind of student evaluation and feedback is needed, and how many books, journal articles, and grants are required in their particular field, if they are to get that first full-time job, acquire tenure, achieve promotion, rise to chair—and what is more, they learn to accept this state of affairs as the norm. Now that continual benchmarking in terms of "excellence" has been introduced, academics are constantly asked to keep a measurable account of everything that happens in their working lives. This includes the number of keynote and plenary lectures they give, the visiting positions they hold, the classes and courses they teach, the leadership they display, and the amount of external income they generate, along with a host of other indicators of the significance, rigor, and originality of their research, its influence, and impact.

A couple of questions are worth raising here. Is all this auditing a way to manage academics in an era when, as Sarah Brouillette puts it in relation to the creative economy, "a spirit of opposition to assigned roles and an openness to change have become crucial facets of the ability to labor successfully" and produce the kind of innovation that leads to economic growth? In such circumstances, does one have to submit to the ceaseless (self-)scrutiny of the management protocols as "a marker of one's commitment to one's work" and self-exploitation?[3] Certainly it is a situation that appears to be at odds with the

3. Sarah Brouillette, *Literature and the Creative Economy* (Stanford, Calif.: Stanford University Press, 2014), 207. For another—albeit perhaps extreme—example of a system of this kind in operation, see the account of life working at Amazon provided in Jodi Kantor and David Streitfeld, "Inside Amazon: Wrestling Big Ideas in a Bruising Workplace," *New York Times,* August 15, 2015, http://www.nytimes.com/2015/08/16/technology/inside -amazon-wrestling-big-ideas-in-a-bruising-workplace.html?_r=1.

way the profession often operates according to something of a "celebrity" approach, whereby, in each field, only a relatively small number of thinkers are deemed "fashionable" on a given topic (i.e., those everyone *must* quote and cite, and whose work thus dominates reading lists and bibliographies). Or at least it *does* until one realizes just how effective this setup is in fostering an acceptance of high levels of intense, individualistic, masculine, neoliberal competition. As Angela McRobbie indicates, drawing on the example of the 9:00 A.M. to 7:00 P.M. working day Thomas Piketty maintains is required to have a successful academic career, it is a model of excellence based on the idea of the brilliant man: someone who can have an enjoyable family life only because he has a wife to provide large amounts of unrecognized domestic support in the form of shopping, cooking, cleaning, and childcare.[4]

The result is that many academics are indeed suffering from stress, anxiety, loneliness, psychological exhaustion, depression, and distress. Yet circumstances will grow markedly worse for this workforce—a high percentage of whom are already in an insecure position—if a shift to a for-profit sharing economy higher education ecosystem occurs, with its ever-present risk to individual teachers of their ratings falling, and even of their being suspended from the platform should they be unable to keep their scores and student acceptance ratio high enough. Such monitoring will be all the more stressful for being never ending, with no final judgment being arrived at—other than suspension or rejection. Rather, these rating systems will act as

4. Angela McRobbie, "Women's Working Lives in the Managerial University and the Pernicious Effects of the 'Normal' Academic Career," *London School of Economics and Political Science: The Impact Blog,* September 3, 2015, http://blogs.lse.ac.uk/impactofsocialsciences/2015/09/03/womens-working-lives-in-the-managerial-university/.

prods by which academics are motivated to *continuously try to do better*. In such a scenario, it will not be long before they begin to act like those microentrepreneurs on eBay who, because their service is constantly being rated, are desperate not to be given any negative feedback on their sales.[5]

That said, ratings systems are far from confined to the online world of platform capitalism. Nowadays, it is not unusual for those working in retail to ask in advance to be given positive feedback if their company has a policy of following up in-store purchases with online requests for customer feedback and a rating of the shopping experience, which almost invariably includes an assessment of the helpfulness of the assistant. In fact, it looks like most individuals in the future will have a reputation score, analogous to their credit rating, based on their online influence and behavior, social connections, and the degree to which they can be trusted, whether they are borrowing money, applying for a job, taking out health insurance, asking for a date, sharing a ride, posting a review, or just leaving a comment.

Again, this may appear something of an exaggeration—yet it, too, is already happening. In November 2014 an anonymous article appeared in the press. It was written by a woman in Germany who purchased tickets for a concert at the Glocke concert hall in Bremen. This woman, the governess of a school in possession of a perfect credit history, discovered that she was unable to arrange a place to stay in the city for the weekend through Airbnb because the website deemed that she had too few friends on Facebook. It turns out that she only had fifty,

5. Lest there be any confusion, I want to make it clear that none of this is to suggest professors should not care about their students or the quality of their teaching. As will become evident later, my point is rather to highlight the antipedagogical nature of this kind of neoliberal audit culture.

whereas she required at least one hundred to verify her online identity and prove she was real to Airbnb—and this despite having booked with a credit card and verified her *offline* identity by scanning in a copy of her driver's license or passport.[6] A "person rating" app called Peeple—described by its developers as "a positive app for positive people"—has even been released that allows users to recommend and review individuals they know on a personal, professional, or romantic basis using a positive–neutral–negative rating system. And before you laugh, such ratings, whereby a person's character is turned into a form of currency, may prove to be increasingly important, because, as Michael Fertik, founder and CEO of Reputation.com, emphasizes, your reputation is tied to that of others in your networks. "The more often your friends default on debt," for example, "the more likely you are to default on debt as well."[7] So if you are thinking of taking out a mortgage and know someone with money troubles, you may want to reconsider your relationship.

Not surprisingly, a number of companies have already been set up to manage people's reputations for them—at a price. (Reputation.com charges a minimum of US$1,050/ £700 a year.) They do so by showing you "what keywords to put in your resume . . . and LinkedIn profile to ensure that you come up at the top of recruiters' and potential employers' search results."[8] They also bombard sites such as Instagram, YouTube,

---

6. "I Didn't Have Enough Facebook Friends to Prove to Airbnb I Was Real," *Guardian,* November 14, 2014, http://www.theguardian .com/money/blog/2014/nov/14/airbnb-wont-let-book-room-facebook -friends. The woman in question kept her name off the article as she was understandably reluctant to broadcast her "official friendlessness" over the Internet.

7. Michael Fertik, *The Reputation Economy* (London: Piatkus, 2015), 172.

8. Ibid., 16.

and Tumblr for you with positive—and mostly bland—content to "create false trails and digital smoke screens." It turns out adopting an interest in cats and top-forty chart music is particularly helpful in this respect. As a result, anything negative or that "doesn't match how you want to be perceived" moves down the rankings of content search engines, making it harder to find and so far less visible.[9] Fifty-three percent of people only pay attention to the first two search results, according to Google, while 89 percent don't make it to the second page.

In the future, are academics going to have to manage *their* reputations too? Are we going to have to put a lot of work into performing sociality with our colleagues, students, peers, and friends on Facebook, Twitter, and Academia.edu to ensure that we maintain a good reputation score?[10] Will we similarly have to feed these platforms with a stream of vanilla, *on-message* content—whatever the academic equivalent of cat pictures is—so as to make anything potentially controversial or overly negative more difficult for platform capitalism's algorithms to discover and highlight?[11]

9. Ibid.

10. The workload is increased by the fact that each platform caters to a different community and uses different tools to produce its ratings and scores. Each platform therefore requires the adoption of a slightly different approach when it comes to reputation management and the performance of sociality.

11. Actually, the academic equivalent of cat pictures may be . . . cat pictures. See both the hashtag #academicswithcats and the *Academia Obscura* blog's Academic Cats Hall of Fame, http://www.academiaobscura .com/academic-cats-hall-of-fame/.

The Microentrepreneur
of the Self

ONE THING IS FOR SURE: achieving a degree of autonomy from these processes of advanced capitalist valorization, modernization, and control by means of a strategic withdrawal of intellectual and bodily labor of the kind championed by the Autonomists—and more recently by Slavoj Žižek—is going to be difficult, if not impossible.[1] Although it is perhaps better suited to the Fordist means of production of the factory with its heavy reliance on *presenteeism,* there is still a certain amount of potential to adopt such a strategy in the public higher education system today, thanks in particular to the protection afforded by state legislation and the unions. Witness the example of Derek Sayer, a professor of cultural history at Lancaster University, who appealed against his *inclusion* in the 2014 Research Excellence Framework (REF), the system by which the quality of research in U.K. higher education institutions is assessed.[2]

1. See Mario Tronti, "The Strategy of Refusal," *Libcom* (blog), July 23, 2005, http://libcom.org/library/strategy-refusal-mario-tronti; Slavoj Žižek, *In Defense of Lost Causes* (London: Verso, 2009).

2. Derek Sayer, "One Scholar's Crusade against the REF," *Times Higher Education,* December 11, 2014, http://www.timeshighereducation

But apart from the fact that, as Sayer's situation demonstrates, such quantification systems are capable of exploiting our labor whether we consciously opt into them or not (just as we are all on Facebook, regardless of whether we have signed up to join its social network), so any freelance individual microentrepreneur who assumes an attitude of noncompliance, nonproductivity, inactivity, laziness, silence, refusal, time wasting, or passive sabotage is unlikely to acquire the kind of rating and reputation score that is needed to retain a gig as an academic in a platform capitalist higher education market. She is quickly going to be found "metrically inadequate," in John Holmwood's memorable phrase.[3]

Faced by such a situation, it is all too easy to imagine fewer and fewer academics being prepared to take a chance on teaching the kind of critically inclined arts and humanities courses that run the risk of being rated as difficult, complex, or otherwise economically unproductive and unviable: say, because they are challenging the status quo (rather than merely servicing it) by exploring *alternative* social, political, and economic visions of the future that are indeed about *more* than work, consumption, and the generation of large profits for someone else to own privately. Instead, academics are likely to prefer to run courses in subjects that are perceived by student debtors-as-consumers as having the potential to help them gain a "good" job with a decent salary. They will thus be involved mainly in producing the

---

.co.uk/features/feature-one-scholars-crusade-against-the-ref/2017405
.fullarticle.

3. John Holmwood, speaking at the Radical Open Access conference, Coventry University, June 15–16, 2015, http://disruptivemedia.org.uk /radical-open-access-conference/. Video recordings of all the talks from the Radical Open Access conference are available at https://archive.org /details/@disruptive_media.

type of unthreatening, lower-level, vocational "workers" that are needed by postwelfare capitalism (and which the current push on the part of many governments toward an "employability agenda" for much of higher education seems determined to generate) rather than the kind of educated public citizens or creative critical thinkers who are capable of maintaining some control over their own work and futures (and who therefore might not be quite so focused on the maximization of production and profit). Any future politicians, business leaders, scientists, or technologists who want an education of that nature will need to attend the kind of "leading" traditional university capable of surviving such disruption.

Yet the for-profit sharing economy acts on far more than the sphere of labor. It acts even on those elements of life that used to be beyond the control of the corporation—underused assets in those most private of spaces, people's homes and cars—but also their sociability, their modes of self-presentation, their personalities. It is not just a political and economic system of management and control, then; it is a psychological one. In fact, the sharing economy is a regime of subjectification designed to produce a specific form of self-preoccupied, self-disciplining subjectivity: that of individuals who function as if they are their own freelance microenterprises. They are individuals who help to generate an environment that produces and valorizes particular modes of behavior by taking responsibility for managing their own employment, learning, health, and well-being in the circumstances created by postwelfare capitalism, with its weakening of social democracy and care. Indeed, because of the degree of surveillance, casualization, and debt they experience, these individuals have little opportunity to act otherwise, having lost the ability to plan and control their own futures. Consequently, they remain personable and positive, even when their way of life is rendered poor and precarious.

In this way, the platform capitalist sharing economy functions to transform us as citizens into connected yet atomized and dispersed individuals who develop our personalities as brands and endeavor to generate social, public, and professional value by acting as both *microentrepreneurs* and *microentrepreneurs of our own selves and lives*.[4] Consequently, the kind of setup I have outlined here regarding the development of an information and data intermediary business model for higher education will affect not just *what* courses academics teach but also *who* teaches them, together with the kind of life they can lead and people they can be. Homophily and the use of rating systems mean it is likely to be only certain individuals who will acquire regular work as academics in the for-profit sharing economy. They will be individuals who are similar to those who use these corporate platforms: who think similar things and are prepared to live and work in similar ways (without defaulting

---

4. In *The Birth of Biopolitics*, Foucault writes of the neoliberal "*homo oeconomicus* as entrepreneur of himself, being for himself his own capital, being for himself his own producer, being for himself the source of [his] earnings." Michel Foucault, *The Birth of Biopolitics: Lectures at the Collège de France, 1978–79* (London: Palgrave Macmillan, 2008), 226. My use of the term *microentrepreneur of the self* here is thus a repurposing of Foucault's neoliberal *homo oeconomicus*, adapted to the context of postwelfare capitalism and the corporate sharing economy. The term *microentrepreneur of the self* is also a play on his concept of "technologies of the self," the general framework of which is very different from the "traditional philosophical questions," for Foucault. It is concerned not with "What is the world? What is man? What is truth? What is knowledge? How can we know something?" but with "What are we in our actuality?" Michel Foucault, "The Political Technology of Individuals," in *Power: Essential Works of Foucault 1954–1984*, vol. 3, ed. James D. Faubion (London: Penguin, 2002), 403. See also Michel Foucault, "Technologies of the Self," in *Technologies of the Self: A Seminar with Michel Foucault*, ed. L. H. Martin, H. Gutman, and P. H. Hutton, 16–49 (London: Tavistock, 1988).

on debt, or ranting against rival supporters in front of a camera crew, as one off-duty lawyer did recently as he left a football match, resulting in the loss of his job with an international law firm). They will also be individuals who are capable of performing the necessary emotional labor to achieve a good student rating: who are smiley, friendly, lighthearted, and "genuine"—or at least capable of appearing to be in what amounts to a kind of forced informality and authenticity—and who are able to mirror the "natural" feel of much social media and so maintain a positive, if largely bland, profile and reputation.

Admittedly, there may be some who see advantages to operating as a freelance academic microentrepreneur for those who can successfully pull it off (and all the more so if they are lucky enough to live in a country with national health provision, an unconditional basic income for everyone, free child care, and other well-developed social safety nets). Doing so may offer more autonomy, independence, and control over the number of hours worked and when, making childcare arrangements easier, for example (although such flexibility has to be put into context: freelancers in the corporate sharing economy still have to operate according to the work allocation, timetable, and conditions set by their respective platform's owners). There will certainly be little or no institutionally generated administration and bureaucracy. Such freelance microentrepreneurs may never again need to deal with a human manager face-to-face. (This is particularly important in view of the fact that having to deal with cab dispatchers and minicab controllers who decide who gets work and who doesn't, often on the basis of favoritism and discrimination, is one reason some drivers have given for switching to Uber.) Nor will there be anything like the same pressure there is now on those in the traditional university system to apply for external funding—money that academics, in the arts and humanities especially, may not actually need for their research but that is required from them by their managers and administrators nonetheless to keep their institutions at the top of the league tables and other metrics. (So-called grant capture is becoming a standard contractual expectation for many at prestigious Russell Group universities in the United Kingdom.) Because CVs and past experience will be less relevant—it is people's work and reputations that will matter now—higher education sharing economy businesses will have the further advantage of providing opportunities for work for those academics who are currently unable to obtain a post in a traditional university (e.g., because they have nontraditional qualifications or life experience; because they are considered to be too old; or because there aren't enough positions available)—or who simply don't want one, perceiving it as too dull and conservative. What is more, a 2015 study of the creative digital IT economy shows that many freelancers are actually paid *more* than their formally employed counterparts.[5]

Significantly, this study is not concerned with freelancers working for the information and data management intermediaries of the sharing economy. Many of the latter are laboring for less than the minimum wage, having lost a host of rights and benefits in the bargain. To be sure, when it comes to higher education, it is unlikely that individual microentrepreneurs will make enough money working for profit-driven postwelfare capitalist businesses to be able to afford to travel regular-

5. Jonathan Sapsed, Roberto Camerani, Monica Masucci, Mylene Petermann, and Megha Rajguru, with Phil Jones, *Brighton Fuse 2: Freelancers in the Creative Digital IT Economy,* January 2015, http://www.brighton fuse.com/wp-content/uploads/2015/01/brighton_fuse2_online.pdf. For an interesting discussion of this research, see David Garcia, "Reframing the Creative Question," February 26, 2015, http://www.nettime.org/.

ly to international conferences—or, indeed, replicate many of the other research-related advantages that come with being employed as a full-time academic in a traditional university. In fact, it is hard to see how research will find much of a place in a for-profit, higher education sharing economy ecosystem at all, especially when the whole point of such an ecosystem will be to offer less expensive teaching while at the same time maximizing the potential for revenue generation. One way of achieving the latter will be by stripping out the cost of paying for all functions other than teaching: precisely activities such as academic research and scholarship, in other words.

The freedom from heavy workloads that provides time for the intellectual contemplation, doubt, curiosity, creative absent-mindedness, idleness, and apparent *inefficacy* that is needed to generate "original" research, certainly in the arts and humanities, is far more likely to be found in the established university system, where the primary goal is education, not profit. (This is why many artists and writers take jobs teaching in a university: as a way of paying their bills and supporting their creative output.) Yet this system is itself becoming increasingly restrictive and is making it more difficult for radical left academics in the arts, humanities, and softer social sciences to find space in which to maneuver, in part because their work does not lend itself quite so readily to being audited and measured and its economic impact assessed as does that of those in the more instrumental and applied harder sciences and quantitative social sciences. Consider the way the U.K. government is using the Research Excellent Framework (REF) and other control mechanisms to ensure (fundamental) research is carried out predominantly in centers of excellence located in the *elite*—what some hold to be the *more* politically and culturally *conservative*—"research intensives," which are themselves becoming "increasingly audit intensive universities."[6] (In such circumstances, the neoliberal drive to reduce "bureaucracy" and "inefficiency" is often used as an alibi for achieving concentration.) Meanwhile, because they are being encouraged to adopt the same values and practices as for-profit corporations (auditing, measurement, division of labor, routinization, casualization, contracting out), universities are themselves shifting much of their attention and resources away from teaching and research to focus on management, marketing, and income generation: "Between 2004 and 2010 the total number of students in UK universities increased by 9%. Over the same period the number of HE managers working in finance, marketing, widening participation, human resources, student services and quality assurance increased by 33%."[7] Indeed, something approaching a symbiotic relationship is apparent here. The more the institutional labor force is encouraged by capitalism and its culture industries to demonstrate a "spirit of opposition to [traditional] assigned roles and an openness to change" by treating work as a form of individual, creative self-development and self-realization (i.e., as an expression of who *they* are as autonomous, flexible, networked individuals), the more this labor force requires an enlarged system of management and bureaucracy to oversee and control it.[8] In turn, those managers and administrators are demanding that academics act as entrepreneurs, both of

6. John Holmwood, "Papering Over the Cracks: The Coming White Paper and the Dismantling of Higher Education," *Campaign for the Public University* (blog), April 25, 2016, http://publicuniversity.org.uk/2016/04/25/papering-over-the-cracks-the-green-paper-and-the-stratification-of-higher-education.

7. Diane Reay, "From Academic Freedom to Academic Capitalism," *Discover Society* (blog), February 15, 2015, http://discoversociety.org/2014/02/15/on-the-frontline-from-academic-freedom-to-academic-capitalism/.

8. Brouillette, *Literature and the Creative Economy*, 207.

themselves and of their research. And one way they are in-sisting academics do so is by bringing in money from exter-nal grants, the applied, practical, monetizable aims of which are steered by government—again putting those in the arts and humanities at a considerable disadvantage compared to their colleagues in science, technology, engineering, and math (STEM)—not least through its role in the appointment of the heads of the research funding bodies. In the context of this shift of focus within the public system of higher education, from teaching and research to academic entrepreneurship and income generation, it is worth noting the following facts as far as the United Kingdom is concerned:

- The Higher Education Funding Council for England is run by the chairman of a real estate firm.
- The Medical Research Council was previously run by a billion-aire arms manufacturer and, since 2012, has been led by the former chairman and chief executive of the investment arm of Barclay's Bank, who also oversaw the disastrous (for the pub-lic purse, at least) privatization of the Royal Mail.
- The Natural Environment Research Council was run by the head of a construction company and, since 2013, has been led by the man who steered AEA Technology plc, which is an offshoot of the U.K. Atomic Energy Authority, through its privatization.[9]

9. This is an updated version of facts first presented in George Monbiot, "These Men Would've Stopped Darwin," *Guardian,* May 11, 2009, http://www.theguardian.com/commentisfree/2009/may/11/science-research-business; see also Reay, "From Academic Freedom to Academic Capitalism."

The Para-academic

ONE ALTERNATIVE for those who wish to produce radical political, critical, or experimental research that is difficult to audit and gain immediate economic impact from (or who just want to have an opportunity to *do less* and *think more*) will be to try to survive by operating on a part-time basis as teachers in the corporate sharing economy or by finding other work to support themselves and their research—much as increasing numbers of musicians are finding that, with record sales falling and there being less money in the music industry, they have to hold down other jobs, even when they have a recording or publishing contract. As Stevphen Shukaitis points out, while once it may have been possible to use music or writing to escape from more regular forms of work, "today it much more seems that it is work which escaped from us, in the sense that there [are only a small] number of decent paying jobs left within publishing and media industries more generally."[1] Is something similar going to happen to those who are employed by universities? Will working solely as an academic and nothing else become largely a thing

1. Stevphen Shukaitis, "Toward an Insurrection of the Published? Ten Thoughts on Ticks and Comrades," European Institute for Progressive Cultural Polices, June 2014, http://eipcp.net/transversal/0614/shukaitis/en.

of the past? To do interesting creative labor, to live a stimulating life comparatively free from postwelfare capitalism's control, surveillance, and deskilling, will they too have to find work outside of the university?

Has a change of this nature not in fact already begun to take place over the course of the last decade or so? I am thinking of those members of the *academic precariat* who, having successfully studied for a postgraduate qualification, might in other eras have expected to acquire a full-time tenured or otherwise permanent position in the academy. What they are finding now, however, is that there is no longer secure—let alone interesting or satisfying—employment to be had in higher education, or even in the arts and cultural industries (museums, art galleries, and so on).[2] So they have developed what Eileen Joy dubs "alt-cult" or "alternate-cultural" organizations and projects that occupy the institutional interstices instead: autonomous universities, schools, presses, journals, and magazines. It is a section of the population that is still interested in scholarly research and ideas—in critical theory, continental philosophy, and so forth—and who often collaborate with those who are employed in higher education on a more secure footing. Only now it is from "the position of the 'para' [the 'beside'], a position of intimate exteriority, or exterior intimacy."[3]

2. For example, "one group of researchers estimates the number of UK-qualified PhDs who do not obtain a permanent academic job within three years is close to 80%, based on a survey of 2505 researchers who had received their PhD in 2010." Sam Moore, "The Practical and Theoretical Foundations for a New Ecosystem of Open-Access Publishing for the Humanities" (PhD thesis, King's College, London, forthcoming), referring to "Some Hard Numbers," *Hortensii* (blog), January 1, 2015, https://hortensii.wordpress.com/2015/01/01/some-hard-numbers/.

3. Eileen Joy, "A Time for Radical Hope: Freedom, Responsibility, Publishing, and Building New Publics," *In the Middle* (blog), November 19, 2013,

The much-vaunted ability of artists to "contest bureaucrat-ic management and other forms of regimentation" is no lon-ger unique today, then, as Brouillette acknowledges. Whether they occupy a position *inside, outside,* or *beside* the university, academics are likewise coming up against the kind of "contra-dictory imperatives" that are a feature of the creative economy. They too are finding themselves in a situation where they are "critical of the institutions that employ them but devoted to the work they [now perhaps *just at times*] do within them; enjoined to make work an expression of who they really are but in cir-cumstances that leave them little time for thought about what that might mean and that ask [them] to package that expres-sion into a readily tradable form."[4] Consider the small "artists" bookshops operating somewhere between the scholarly and trade markets that have appeared in cities such as Los Angeles, London, and Amsterdam in recent years to cater to this demo-graphic. It is also this para-academic community that the "radi-cal press" Zero Books, an imprint of John Hunt Publishing Ltd., is appealing to.[5] "Intellectual without being academic, popular

---

http://www.inthemedievalmiddle.com/2013/11/a-time-for-radical-hope -freedom.html#sthash.s5ZcU46o.dpuf. For more on the para-academic, see Alex Wardrop and Deborah Withers, eds., *The Para-Academic Handbook* (Bristol, U.K.: HammerOn Press, 2014).

4. Brouillette, *Literature and the Creative Economy,* 207.

5. I put "radical press" in quotation marks because, although the content of what Zero Books publishes may be radical, its business model is not. This is something that one of its founders, Tariq Goddard, emphasized to me in the question-and-answer session that followed his presentation at the November 2014 Post-Digital Scholar conference in Leuphana, Germany (https://hybridpublishing.org/postdigital-scholar-conference/). Meanwhile, Eileen Joy, who is the editor of another para-academic press, Punctum Books, has summed up the somewhat contradictory nature of Zero Books's philosophy as follows: "while Zero Books, indeed, offers a particularly electric and eclectic list of reasonably-priced, shorter-form

without being populist," as the mission statement printed at the back of each of its volumes puts it, Zero Books is particularly fashionable among para-academics, being somewhere they can publish shorter-form, reasonably priced books on radical theory, philosophy, and politics. Zero has a comparatively quick turnaround, in large part because John Hunt Publishing doesn't insist on spending as much time and money as a more traditional academic press on providing services such as rigorous editorial input, copy editing, and peer review.[6] Yet, as a publisher of

books (*Slime Dynamics, Nuclear Futurism,* and *Levitate the Primate* are just a few samples of their bracing titles), they do not offer any of their publications in open-access form. Thus, their desire for a reinvigorated and non-bland, non-consensual sphere of public intellectual debate is still somewhat in the shadow of the multinational corporations (such as Amazon.com, to which all of their book pages link) that their mission statement scorns." Eileen Joy, "All in a Jurnal's Work: A BABEL Wayzgoose," *Punctum Books* (blog), February 15, 2013, http://punctumbooks.com/blog /all-in-a-jurnals-work-a-babel-wayzgoose. Zero Books thus illustrates how even that produced by those edgy nonconformists who inhabit the less obviously controlled interstices of the formal institutional and corporate domains can serve as potential material for capitalist exploitation, and how capital can count on a supply of this material, even while refusing to finance its production by providing secure employment in the higher education and creative industries sectors.

Does this explain why a number of established academics who *are* employed full time in a traditional university are also publishing with Zero? The appeal has to do not just with the degree of intellectual freedom and quick turnaround time Zero Books offers but also with the fact that Zero Books is different in the sense many academics want—having an air of edginess and nonconformism about it—but not *so very different* that publishing with Zero will actually challenge these academics and the way they live, work, and think (in terms of copyright, IP, fixity, the finished object, etc.).

6. Details of the publishing process of Zero Books are available on its website, http://www.zero-books.net/publishing-process.html, and that of John Hunt Publishing, https://www.johnhuntpublishing

"critical and engaged" intellectual work, the lack of such man-
datory services does not do Zero as much reputational harm as
it might have done in previous eras. This is because extensive
copy editing and peer review are nowhere near as important to
the current generation of para-academics as they are to those
who are more firmly ensconced within the institution of the
university and who still need them for professional reasons to
do with academic legitimation and accreditation.

.com/jhp-publishing-process.html. All proposals submitted get several
very short Reader Reports for which authors are not charged, while all
manuscripts accepted for publication receive a "light edit." Anything
more than that is optional and charged for. This includes "a longer, 500–
1000 word evaluation" of the proposal, a "more detailed evaluation of
the manuscript, with suggestions for improvement, 3000–5000 words,"
and a "heavy edit" to enforce the style manual and correct typos,
spelling, grammar, and general punctuation mistakes.

The Artrepreneur

THERE IS THUS A VERY REAL DANGER that the range of those who have an opportunity to create, publish, and disseminate *adventurous*—what we might today call *brave*—political or critical scholarship and research may grow even narrower in the future. If much of the publicly funded, nonprofit university system is disrupted by the higher education information and data intermediaries of the sharing economy (and is becoming a less hospitable place for radical arts and humanities academics to work anyway), and if these for-profit platform capitalist businesses provide little direct support for research themselves, the writing of scholarly books and journal articles will be restricted increasingly to those who are acceptable to the forces of the market—or at least those parts of the market that are willing and able to provide authors with sufficient income to buy them time for their research. If this income is to be gained from their writing, it means far greater emphasis will be placed on producing articles, trade books, introductions, textbooks, and reference works that have the potential to garner a wide nonacademic readership. Even entering these more publicly accessible sectors of the market may not be enough to ensure that one has an opportunity to write and be published, however. According to the Zero Books website, approximately "one quarter of the titles on the list have an element of subsidy from the author, where the readers/editors liked the book but were not confident that [they] would recover the publishing costs."[1] Taken together, it is a set of circumstances that risks creating a situation in which only those who are already comfortable financially can afford to be critical of capitalism.

Does this mean that academics who produce radical, critical, or avant-garde work (i.e., research that is often unpredictable and noncalculable) will have to look to very different sources of funding and support, much as many in the art world are doing? The Louis Vuitton Foundation recently opened an arts center in Paris, designed by Frank Gehry, while the Prada Foundation has opened one in Milan, this time designed by Rem Koolhaas. So we have privately owned companies, making their money from the sale of luxury goods, starting to fill the gaps left by the withdrawal of public funding. What these companies receive in turn is an enrichment of their brand and an extension of their reach into new spheres of society. Is something of this kind actually possible for the kind of critical work many arts and humanities academics are interested in? Even if it were (and of course there are numerous examples of cultural philanthropy being shown by previous generations of capitalists), would it not require them to again become, at best, entrepreneurs of themselves and of their research, much as "artist-entrepreneurs" such as Jeff Koons, Tracey Emin, and Grayson Perry have become their own celebrity brands through their blurring of the boundaries between fine art and

1. http://www.zero-books.net/about-us.html, accessed July 19, 2015. This figure has since been reduced. At the time of this writing (July 3, 2016), the Zero Books website claims that only approximately 10 percent of its titles are subsidized by authors.

luxury labels?[2] As such, would it not discourage risk by rewarding primarily those who are able to deliver works that are recognizable as part of their brand identity on a regular basis, just as the art market does with regard to high-value artists now?

Another option—one that has become available to authors only in the last decade or so—will be to try to appeal to enough people who are prepared to pay a small amount each to see a book brought to publication under the kind of crowd-funding model that is championed by Kickstarter (which has attracted $2 billion in pledges since it launched in 2009), Unbound, and Readership. The latter describes itself as a "digital book publisher controlled by readers." Writers first upload extracts of their work. Readers then vote *yes* or *no* and accompany each *yes* vote with a financial donation. Readership publishes every book that reaches its financial target.[3] However, the crowd-funding model represents not so much an alternative to free market capitalism as an extension of it. Basically, it functions as a "reverse market with prepaid investment," as Michel Bauwens and Vasilis Kostakis describe it. Rather than "going to the banks for money" to set up the business, the crowd-funded publisher and author simply go to the people.[4]

2. See Giulia Zaniol's solo exhibition and public forum parodying celebrity art and luxury branding, *Brand Art Sensation: A Mass Debate,* Gallery Different, London, June 9–13, 2015, http://www.zaniol.com/eminent.

3. http://readershipbooks.com/Home/About.

4. Indeed, Bauwens and Kostakis go so far as to quote Mike Bulajewski's description of Kickstarter, in particular, as "the very definition of parasitic capitalism," in that it is actually a "sophisticated web hosting provider which charges '60 times the actual cost of providing a service by skimming a percentage off financial transactions.'" Michael Bauwens and Vasilis Kostakis, *Network Society and Future Scenarios for a Collaborative Economy* (London: Palgrave Pivot, 2014).

Moreover, what if our research is *not* designed to provide prospective readers with what they already know they want—or think they know they want—and are thus willing to pay for, either pre- or postpublication? What if we wish to produce work that does not necessarily have a predefined audience or market it is trying to appeal to?

Affirmative Disruption

IN A 1983 ARTICLE for *Le Monde* called "The Tomb of the Intellectual," the philosopher Jean-François Lyotard responds to a plea from the French government for intellectuals to have a "concrete involvement" with thinking on economic and social matters.[1] Given that we are facing similar calls from governments today for our research to have the kind of impact that changes the behavior of its addressees, what is so interesting about this article is that philosophers *are not* intellectuals, according to Lyotard, in that they do not identify with, nor endeavor to speak for, a universal subject, be it "man, humanity, the nation, the people, the proletariat."[2] Nor are philosophers *experts* whose role is to achieve the best possible "input/output (cost/benefit)" performance ratio in their preconstituted fields. (It is the experts—ideas people, decision makers, those who have specific administrative, economic, social, and cultural responsibilities—that the French government is really appealing to when it calls for thinkers to have a concrete impact.) Along with artists and writers, Lyotard assigns philosophers instead to a third category: that of

1. Jean-François Lyotard, "The Tomb of the Intellectual," in *Jean-François Lyotard: Political Writings* (London: UCL Press, 2003), 3.
2. Ibid.

"creator" or experimenter.[3] As such, they are responsible only to the question "what is painting, writing, thought?"[4] In contrast to experts, experimenters therefore remain unperturbed by the notion that the vast majority of people may not readily understand what they do. They are unconcerned by this notion because they do not have a pregiven addressee, whether this be known as a "public," "readership," "audience," or "market," that they are trying to win over and seduce. Rather, philosophers, artists, and writers are by definition involved in questioning the limits of preconstituted fields—along with the accepted criteria of judgment (i.e., of performativity, of "what works best") by which they would be held to account if they were to be criticized for not being intelligible, useful, profitable, or political enough.

(Lyotard)

Of course, Lyotard was writing in a different time and place. Yet what if, in the era of platform capitalist higher education, we too wish to produce "troublesome, impossible" research that is engaged in questioning the "received compartmentalization of realities and . . . criterion for the evaluation of actions" on which any public, readership, audience, market, or indeed "crowd" that preexists this research and can be generated around it might be based?[5] In that case, will we not have to try to create performatively the very economy in which such research can find funding and support?

To approach this issue from a slightly different angle, how might we in turn *disrupt the disruptors* of public, nonprofit higher education, with a view to inventing a different, more

3. Ibid., 5. "Experimenter" is the term Geoffrey Bennington suggests on the grounds that it "avoids the Christian overtones of 'creator.'" Bennington, *Lyotard: Writing the Event* (Manchester, U.K.: Manchester University Press, 1988), 6.

4. Lyotard, "Tomb of the Intellectual," 4.

5. Ibid., 7, 4.

caring future: for academic labor, for the sharing economy, even for advanced postindustrial society? Thus far, I have primarily used the term *disruption* in the widely adopted Silicon Valley sense, which, although it may be derived from it, is not quite the same as the theory of technological disruption of Clayton Christensen and his colleagues at the Harvard Business School. A disruptive technology, for Christensen, as laid out in his book *The Innovator's Dilemma,* is one that typically facilitates the production of a new market for products and services and eventually succeeds in disrupting an already existing market. So, to return to the subject of transport, in the 1960s and 1970s, Honda's introduction of small off-road motorcycles to the North American market disrupted established, over-the-road motorbike manufacturers such as Harley-Davidson. Christensen's argument is that organizations "entering these markets early have strong first-mover advantages over later entrants." The problem is, as these organizations "succeed and grow larger, it becomes progressively difficult for them to enter the even newer small markets [that are] destined to become the large ones in the future," which means they are themselves likely to be disrupted eventually by other, fresher upstart organizations.[6] This is because of what Christensen calls the "innovator's dilemma," whereby, for reasons of institutionalization, "companies find it very difficult to invest adequate resources in disruptive technologies—lower-margin technologies that their customers don't want—until their customers want them. And by then it is too late."[7]

6. Clayton M. Christensen, *The Innovator's Dilemma: When New Technologies Cause Great Firms to Fail* (Cambridge, Mass.: Harvard Business School Press, 1997), xx.

7. Ibid., xix.

While Uber may be an innovation that is disruptive in the looser Silicon Valley sense (as for convenience's sake I have been terming it), in that it threatens to transform the taxi industry and put many previously successful cab companies out of business, it is not strictly speaking a genuinely disruptive innovation according to Christensen's theory. This is because, as Christensen makes clear in a recent coauthored article for *Harvard Business Review,* Uber does not have its origins in either "low-end or new-market footholds":

> It is difficult to claim that the company found a low-end opportunity: that would have meant taxi service providers had overshot the needs of a material number of customers by making cabs too plentiful, too easy to use and too clean. Neither did Uber primarily target non-consumers—people who found the existing alternatives so expensive or inconvenient that they took public transit or drove themselves instead: Uber was launched in San Francisco (a well-served taxi market), and Uber's customers were generally people already in the habit of hiring rides.[8]

In fact, whereas "disrupters *start* by appealing to low-end or unserved consumers and then migrate to the mainstream market," Uber has done precisely the opposite. It has begun by creating a "less expensive solution to a widespread customer need" in the mainstream market, before proceeding to appeal to segments of the market that have been overlooked historically.[9] For Christensen et al., Uber is thus much more of a sustaining innovation than a disruptive innovation, in that it is making what customers already consider a good product even better.

---

8. Clayton M. Christensen, Michael E. Raynor, and Rory McDonald, "What Is Disruptive Innovation?," *Harvard Business Review,* December 2015, https://hbr.org/2015/12/what-is-disruptive-innovation.
9. Ibid.

I want to emphasize, however, that I am not interested in the process of disruption for the reasons Christensen and Silicon Valley are interested in it: as a way of understanding innovation-driven economic growth to show how it is possible to succeed as a disruptive innovator, that is, as "a smaller company with fewer resources" that is able to "successfully challenge established incumbent businesses."[10] It is not my intention to try to sustain and develop the current capitalist economic system, its overall logic, modes, and relations of production, by playing up the potential of disruptive technologies to generate innovations that are capable of facilitating the creation of a new market while at the same time playing down the destructive effects of these technologies. Rather than helping capitalism to constantly renew itself with what Joseph Schumpeter, building on the economic theory of Karl Marx, understands as waves of "creative destruction," my interest is in disrupting the free market itself by using such technologies to experiment with the invention of *new* economies and *new* economic models. This is why I am using the term "affirmative disruption" here—to mark this difference. I am employing this concept in the sense in which Roberto Esposito writes of an "affirmative biopolitics" in relation to the work of Michel Foucault, where an "affirmative biopolitics" is "one that is not defined negatively with respect to the dispositifs of modern power/knowledge but is rather situated along the line of tension that traverses and displaces them."[11]

10. Ibid.

11. Roberto Esposito, *The Third Person: Politics of Life and Philosophy of the Impersonal* (London: Polity, 2012), 18. Esposito writes, "Life, one might say, is a biological stratum that, for Foucault, is never coextensive with subjectivity because it is always caught in a dual, simultaneous process of subjection and subjectification: it is the space that power lays siege

At the same time, it is important to be aware that *affirmatively disrupting the disruptors* of public, nonprofit higher education will require us to *revolutionize* more than the instruments and relations of production, that is, the way in which we work.[12] After all, aggressive, global, for-profit technology companies such as Amazon, Google, Uber, and Airbnb are concerned not just with what we *do* but with who we *are*. Capital and life (bios) are intertwined, in other words—to the point where *we are* the very neoliberal microenterprises we will be trying to creatively destroy and experimentally place in question. Affirmatively disrupting the postwelfare capitalism of the sharing economy will thus mean affirmatively disrupting the microentrepreneurs of our own selves and lives we have become.

---

to without ever managing to occupy it fully" (18). A further articulation of an *affirmative* approach to disruption can be found in Pauline Van Mourik Broekman, Gary Hall, Ted Byfield, Shaun Hides, and Simon Worthington, *Open Education: A Study in Disruption* (London: Rowman and Littlefield International, 2014).

12. See Karl Marx and Friedrich Engels, *The Communist Manifesto*, 1848, in *Marx/Engels Selected Works*, vol. 1 (Moscow: Progress, 1969), available as *Manifesto of the Communist Party by Karl Marx and Frederick Engels*, Marxists Internet Archive, 16, http://www.marxists.org/archive /marx/works/1848/communist-manifesto. For more on this point, see Gary Hall, *Pirate Philosophy: For a Digital Posthumanities* (Cambridge, Mass.: MIT Press, 2016).

Postscript

IT IS WITH THE ENACTMENT of such an affirmative disruption of the ways in which we live, work, and think—not only as neoliberals but as liberals too—that I have been experimenting in recent years. I have been doing so along with a number of different actors, groups, and organizations, some of which operate under the names of *Culture Machine,* Open Humanities Press, and the Centre for Disruptive Media.[1] The result has been a series of performative media projects—*performative* in the sense that they are concerned not so much with representing the world (or not *just* with doing so) as with *acting in* or *intra-acting with* it.[2] They include Media Gifts, the Liquid Books series, Liquid

1. See *Culture Machine,* http://www.culturemachine.net/; Open Humanities Press, http://openhumanitiespress.org/; Centre for Disruptive Media, http://disruptivemedia.org.uk/.

2. In *Meeting the Universe Halfway,* Karen Barad writes, "The agential realist approach that I offer eschews representationalism and advances a performative understanding of technoscientific and other naturalcultural practices, including different kinds of knowledge-making practices. According to agential realism, knowing, thinking, measuring, theorizing, and observing are material practices of intra-acting within and as part of the world." Barad, *Meeting the Universe Halfway: Quantum Physics and the Entanglement of Matter and Meaning* (Durham, N.C.:

Theory TV, *Photomediations Machine,* and *Photomediations: An Open Book.*[3] *The Uberfication of the University* is part of an expanded, iterative text involved in creating just such a performative media project, the aim of which is to affirmatively disrupt platform capitalism and the corporate sharing economy.

Duke University Press, 2007), 90–91. In this respect, Barad prefers the notion of *intra-action* to that of interaction, seeing the latter as presuming "the prior existence of independent entities/relata." Karen Barad, "Posthumanist Performativity: Toward an Understanding of How Matter Comes to Matter," *Signs: Journal of Women in Culture and Society* 28, no. 3 (2003): 815. As such, she considers intra-action to represent "a profound conceptual shift" (815). Similarly, for her, the move toward performative alternatives to representationalism shifts the focus from questions of correspondence between descriptions and reality (e.g., do they mirror nature or culture?) to matters of "practices/doings/actions" (802).

    3. See Media Gifts, http://garyhall.squarespace.com/about/; the Liquid Books series, http://liquidbooks.pbwiki.com/; Liquid Theory TV, http://www.culturemachine.net/index.php/cm/article/view/354/358; *Photomediations Machine,* http://photomediationsmachine.net; and *Photomediations: An Open Book,* http://www.photomediationsopen book.net/.

Acknowledgments

I would like to thank Joanna Zylinska, Kathleen Fitzpatrick, John Holmwood, and Clare Birchall for their comments on earlier versions of this book and some of the ideas it contains. Special thanks are due to John Holmwood for initially inviting me to write about the uberfication of the university for *Discover Society*.

Gary Hall is research professor of media and performing arts at Coventry University, United Kingdom. He is author of *Culture in Bits* (2002), *Digitize This Book!* (Minnesota, 2008), and *Pirate Philosophy* (2016). In 1999, he cofounded the journal *Culture Machine,* and in 2006, he cofounded Open Humanities Press.